YOUR KNOWLEDGE HAS VALUE

Is Anybody Out There? The Impact of Trust in Virtual Teams

Sabina Dörner

Bibliographic information published by the German National Library:

The German National Library lists this publication in the National Bibliography; detailed bibliographic data are available on the Internet at http://dnb.dnb.de.

ISBN: 9783346608161
This book is also available as an ebook.

Is Anybody Out There?

The Impact of Trust in Virtual Teams

Maastricht University

School of Business and Economics

Dörner, S.

SBE Pre-Master

Academic Writing Skills

Maastricht, 24 May 2021

Critical Literature Review

2

Table of Contents

1. Introduction

Over the past two decades, megatrends such as digitalisation, globalisation, and technological evolution have shaped the nature of work (Großer & Baumöl, 2017). In response, a growing number of organisations are shifting from traditional to virtual environments (Gilson et al., 2015). Organisations are increasingly implementing teams that collaborate online across national, cultural, and organisational boundaries using communication technologies (Hacker et al., 2019). One study reveals that the number of employees working in virtual settings increased by 173 percent between 2005 and 2018 (Global Workplace Analytics, 2020). In 2018, 18 percent of the global workforce worked virtually full-time (Owl Labs, 2018), but that number rose to 69 percent by 2020 (Owl Labs, 2020). Virtual collaboration has increased largely due to the COVID-19 pandemic, as it requires organisations to enable remote working (Mysirlaki & Paraskeva, 2020). Scholars estimate that 73 percent of teams will operate at least partially in virtual settings by 2028 (Upwork, 2019). Accordingly, virtual teams have become an integral part of corporate structures (Hacker et al., 2019).

While virtual collaboration has benefits, it also poses challenges that virtual teams must face to be effective (Mysirlaki & Paraskeva, 2020). As Gibson and Cohen (2003) explain, building trust among team members is challenging due to the lack of face-to-face interaction and technology-based communication in virtual relationships. However, trust within teams is crucial for their effectiveness (Breuer et al., 2016). Therefore, the purpose of this paper is to investigate the impact of trust on virtual team effectiveness.

Firstly, this paper defines virtual teams and introduces the concept of virtual team effectiveness. Secondly, it examines the impact of trust on virtual team effectiveness. Finally, it points out implications for virtual managers on how to build trust in virtual teams and gives recommendations for future research.

2. Virtual Teams

The following section defines virtual teams and distinguishes them from traditional teams by conceptualizing virtuality in teamwork. Furthermore, it elaborates on the concept of virtual team effectiveness and explains its complex nature.

2.1 Definition

As virtual teams have gained popularity in recent years, various approaches to their definition have emerged in the literature (Ale Ebrahim et al., 2009). Based on the most commonly identified characteristics, the authors define virtual teams as co-workers that rely on technology-mediated communication to cooperate across geographical locations, time zones, and organisational structures toward a shared objective. Due to the spatial distance, virtual team members communicate electronically rather than face-to-face (Mehta & Shah, 2019). To do so, they use digital means, such as video conferencing, file transfer, and application sharing (Morrison-Smith & Ruiz, 2020).

Early literature suggests that virtual teams differ from conventional teams by their geographic dispersion and use of technology (Gilson et al., 2015). However, during the COVID-19 pandemic, more and more team members have been cooperating virtually without being geographically dispersed (Zeuge et al., 2020). Moreover, teams working together on-site may also use communication technologies (Dulebohn & Hoch, 2017). Therefore, studies have recently taken a more multidimensional approach to conceptualize virtuality (Hacker et al,

2019). Jimenez et al. (2017) conclude that virtuality is determined not solely by spatial distance, but also by temporal and structural dispersion in terms of economic, educational, and demographic backgrounds. Kirkman and Mathieu (2005) specify virtuality based on the use of technology. As they point out, virtual teams utilize digital communication tools more intensively to accomplish tasks and exchange valuable information than conventional teams (Kirkman & Mathieu, 2005). Taken together, the concept of virtuality encompasses whether teams are dispersed across multiple dimensions and the extent to which they apply communication technologies (Jimenez et al., 2017; Kirkman & Mathieu, 2005).

2.2 Virtual Team Effectiveness

Teams strive to perform their tasks effectively. However, team effectiveness is a complex and multidimensional concept (Pangil & Chan, 2014). Ross et al. (2008) note that team effectiveness relates to its performance, behaviour, and attitude. Lin et al. (2008) define team effectiveness based on the team member's performance and satisfaction. Although the existing literature elaborates on the concept of team effectiveness, little attention has been paid to the effectiveness of virtual teams in particular (Pangil & Chan, 2014). Pangil and Chan (2014) argue that despite the differences between virtual and conventional teams, both are expected to achieve goals. Hence, virtual team effectiveness can also be determined by the team member's performance and satisfaction (Pangil & Chan, 2014).

Due to the complexity of team effectiveness, the outcomes of virtual teams are difficult to assess (Gilson et al., 2015). Some studies report that virtual teams are more effective than conventional teams (Maynard et al., 2012), while other studies indicate that working virtually decreases effectiveness (Schweitzer & Duxbury, 2010). Previous research has explored various factors that affect whether or not virtual teams succeed. However, few studies have focused on the variables that determine virtual team effectiveness (Pangil & Chan, 2014). These studies conclude that influential factors are knowledge sharing (Pangil & Chan, 2014), trust (Brahm & Kunze, 2012), technology (Berry, 2011), communication (Jong et al., 2008), and leadership (Hoch & Kozlowski, 2014).

3. Trust in Virtual Teams

Among the factors influencing effectiveness, prior research identifies trust as critical to virtual team functioning (Brahm & Kunze, 2012). Jong et al. (2016) describe trust within teams as the shared perception of reliance among team members. It reflects the extent to which team members trust each other in terms of integrity, fairness, and reliability (Berry, 2011). When team members trust each other, they are confident that each member will make commitments and behave in the team's best interests (Morrison-Smith & Ruiz, 2020).

Effective teamwork is based on trust among team members (Breuer et al., 2016). Virtual team members are more dependent on each other due to the lack of coordination and control mechanisms and non-verbal communication in their interaction (Morrison-Smith & Ruiz, 2020; Shin, 2004). In trusting working environments, team members support each other, exchange feedback, and address conflicts. Moreover, trust fosters team commitment and effective group functioning (Morrison-Smith & Ruiz, 2020). In their research, Jong et al. (2016) show that high-trusting teams perform better. Similarly, Brahm and Kunze (2012) establish that members of such teams are more confident in their relationships and interactions with other members, which enhances team cohesion. Therefore, mutual trust is crucial for people working together virtually to function effectively as a team (Brahm & Kunze, 2012).

Building and maintaining trust in virtual environments is challenging, however (Pangil & Chan, 2014). Limited face-to-face contact makes it difficult to develop solid relationships. The lack of non-verbal and contextual information in technology-mediated communication and the anonymity of the communication channels are also barriers to establishing personal connections (Gibson & Cohen, 2003). Additionally, virtual teams communicate less frequently and synchronously due to temporal and geographical dispersion. However, building trust requires frequent and intensive interaction (Pangil & Chan, 2014). Similarly, the diversity of virtual teams can create language barriers and lead to cultural differences, which can hinder communication and team identification (Krawczyk-Bryłka, 2016). Collectively, these studies indicate that establishing trust is a challenge for virtual teams due to spatial distance, technology-based communication, and different cultural backgrounds (Gibson & Cohen, 2003).

4. Building Trust in Virtual Teams

As previously discussed, trust plays a critical role in virtual team effectiveness and yet is difficult to develop in virtual teams. Therefore, virtual managers need to understand how to build trust within their teams (Pangil & Chan, 2014). Lukić and Vračar (2018) suggest that managers can establish a basis for trust in the recruitment and selection process for virtual team members. Managers should not only focus on the employee's job-related skills but also on their personal characteristics and propensity to trust (Greenberg et al., 2007). Ford et al. (2017) identify valuable traits of virtual team members: Willingness to trust, proficiency with the technology used, and good self-management and communication skills. To work successfully in a virtual team, team members should also have high integrity, cultural sensitivity, and interpersonal skills (Lukić & Vračar, 2018). By properly assembling virtual teams, managers can facilitate the development of trust (Greenberg et al., 2007).

When team members are first assigned to teams, they rely on external sources to build a sense of trust that allows them to begin collaborating (Greenberg et al., 2007). Managers should develop behavioural norms that guide team members in their interaction with each other (Lukić & Vračar, 2018). They should also clearly define the expectations and responsibilities of all members to avoid possible misunderstandings (Ale Ebrahim et al., 2009). By communicating those, team members learn what they can expect from each other (Lukić & Vračar, 2018). According to Ford et al. (2017), trust can also be built through organisational practices such as training or onboarding, which familiarise team members with their colleagues. To do so, managers must introduce team members to each other and provide opportunities for them to know each other (Ford et al., 2017). For the latter, they can schedule face-to-face meetings early in the collaboration, which facilitates trust development. Another option is to conduct online team-building activities that focus on self-disclosure. Sharing personal information helps to build stronger relationships and create team cohesiveness (Ferrell & Kline, 2018). By adopting these practices, managers can create a trusting environment for virtual teams (Lukić & Vračar, 2018).

After establishing a framework, managers should focus on communication processes (Gibson & Cohen, 2003). Pangil and Chan (2014) show that frequent communication and information exchange reduces the uncertainty and anonymity of digital communication means. Therefore, managers would benefit from organizing weekly meetings through video-based communication tools as they also transmit non-verbal and contextual information (Ferrell & Kline, 2018). Moreover, managers should recognize that high-trust environments require timely responses, valuable feedback, and open communication (Henttonen & Blomqvist, 2005). Gibson and Cohen (2003) highlight the importance of a supportive communication climate where failure is allowed, and conflicts are resolved fairly and openly. In this regard, managers must encourage team members to be open to new approaches and embrace innovation. They can do this by openly showing support for people who have taken risks with unconventional ideas, regardless of their success (Gibson & Cohen, 2003). In sum, virtual teams can develop trust if they communicate frequently and openly, receive useful feedback, and are supportive (Gibson & Cohen, 2003; Henttonen & Blomqvist, 2005).

5. Conclusion

Organizations are increasingly deploying virtual teams to meet technological and societal developments. However, virtual teams face the challenge of building trust, which is crucial for team effectiveness. To establish a foundation for trust, managers must consider the team member's characteristics and skills when assembling the team. For this purpose, it is also important that they clearly define the behavioural norms, expectations, and responsibilities of each member. In the onboarding process, managers should provide opportunities for team members to know each other to create a sense of familiarity and team cohesiveness, which can be achieved through face-to-face meetings or online team-building activities. Moreover, open and regular communication between team members fosters a trusting environment. It is also beneficial for managers to provide valuable feedback and create a supportive communication climate. With these measures, managers can establish and maintain trust within virtual teams and thus increase their effectiveness.

This literature review has explained the impact of trust on virtual team effectiveness and how trust can be developed in virtual work environments. However, this paper has potential limitations. The literature reviewed here is written exclusively in English and covers only a period of 17 years. This review also relies entirely on previously published studies and their availability. Future research could verify the findings by conducting a comprehensive study that links the results to empirical evidence. Further studies might also explore different types of trust and their impact on virtual teams. Additionally, they could investigate how to foster trust in already established teams transitioning from traditional to virtual environments. By developing trust in virtual teams, organizations can foster effective collaboration that provides them with a sustainable competitive advantage in the increasingly dynamic and disruptive business environments.

11

References

Ale Ebrahim, N., Ahmed, S., & Taha, Z. (2009). Virtual teams: A literature

review. *Australian Journal of Basic and Applied Sciences, 3*(3), 2653-2669.

Berry, G. R. (2011). Enhancing effectiveness on virtual teams: Understanding why traditional

team skills are insufficient. *Journal of Business Communication, 48*(2), 186-206.

https://doi.org/10.1177/0021943610397270

Brahm, T., & Kunze, F. (2012). The role of trust climate in virtual teams. *Journal of*

Managerial Psychology, 27(6), 595-614. https://doi.org/10.1108/02683941211252446

Breuer, C., Hüffmeier, J., & Hertel, G. (2016). Does Trust Matter More in Virtual Teams? A

Meta-Analysis of Trust and Team Effectiveness Considering Virtuality and

Documentation as Moderators. *Journal of Applied Psychology, 101*(8), 1151-1177.

https://doi.org/10.1037/apl0000113

Dulebohn, J. H., & Hoch, J. E. (2017). Virtual teams in organizations. *Human Resource*

Management Review, 27(4), 569-574. https://doi.org/10.1016/j.hrmr.2016.12.004

Ferrell, J., & Kline, K. (2018). Facilitating trust and communication in virtual teams. *People*

& Strategy, 41(2), 30-36.

Ford, R. C., Piccolo, R. F., & Ford, L. R. (2017). Strategies for building effective virtual

teams: Trust is key. *Business Horizons, 60*(1), 25-34.

https://doi.org/10.1016/j.bushor.2016.08.009

Gibson, C. B., & Cohen, S. G. (2003). *Virtual teams that work: Creating conditions for

virtual team effectiveness.* John Wiley & Sons.

Gilson, L. L., Maynard, M. T., Jones Young, N. C., Vartiainen, M., & Hakonen, M. (2015).

Virtual Teams Research: 10 Years, 10 Themes, and 10 Opportunities. *Journal of

Management, 41*(5), 1313-1337. https://doi.org/10.1177/0149206314559946

Global Workplace Analytics (2020, March 13). *Latest Work-At-Home/Telecommuting/Mobile

Work/Remote Work Statistics.* https://globalworkplaceanalytics.com/telecommuting-

statistics

Greenberg, P. S., Greenberg, R. H., & Antonucci, Y. L. (2007). Creating and sustaining trust

in virtual teams. *Business Horizons, 50*(4), 325-333.

https://doi.org/10.1016/j.bushor.2007.02.005

Großer, B., & Baumöl, U. (2017). Virtual teamwork in the context of technological and

cultural transformation. *International Journal of Information Systems and Project

Management, 5*(4), 21-35. http://dx.doi.org/10.12821/ijispm050402

Hacker, J. V., Johnson, M., Saunders, C., & Thayer, A. L. (2019). Trust in virtual teams: A multidisciplinary review and integration. *Australasian Journal of Information Systems*, *23*, 1-36. https://doi.org/10.3127/ajis.v23i0.1757

Henttonen, K., & Blomqvist, K. (2005). Managing distance in a global virtual team: the evolution of trust through technology-mediated relational communication. *Strategic Change*, *14*(2), 107-119. https://doi.org/10.1002/jsc.714

Hoch, J. E., & Kozlowski, S. W. (2014). Leading virtual teams: Hierarchical leadership, structural supports, and shared team leadership. *Journal of Applied Psychology*, *99*(3), 390-403. https://doi.org/10.1037/a0030264

Jimenez, A., Boehe, D. M., Taras, V., & Caprar D. V. (2017). Working Across Boundaries: Current and Future Perspectives in Global Virtual Teams. *Journal of International Management, 23*(4), 341-349. https://doi.org/10.1016/j.intman.2017.05.001

Jong, B. A. de., Dirks, K. T., & Gillespie, N. (2016). Trust and team performance: A meta-analysis of main effects, moderators, and covariates. *Journal of Applied Psychology, 101*(8), 1134–1150. https://doi.org/10.1037/apl0000110

Jong, R. de., Schalk, R., & Curşeu, P. L. (2008). Virtual communicating, conflicts and performance in teams. *Team Performance Management, 14(7/8),* 364-380. https://doi.org/10.1108/13527590810912331

Kirkman, B. L., & Mathieu, J. E. (2005). The dimensions and antecedents of team

virtuality. *Journal of Management, 31*(5), 700-718.

https://doi.org/10.1177/0149206305279113

Krawczyk-Bryłka, B. (2016). Intercultural Challenges in Virtual Teams. *Journal of*

Intercultural Management, 8(3), 69-85. https://doi.org/10.1515/joim-2016-0017

Lin, C., Standing, C., & Liu, Y. C. (2008). A model to develop effective virtual

teams. *Decision Support Systems, 45*(4), 1031-1045.

https://doi.org/10.1016/j.dss.2008.04.002

Lukić, J. M., & Vračar, M. M. (2018). Building and nurturing trust among members in virtual

project teams. *Strategic Management, 23*(3), 10-16.

https://doi.org/10.5937/straman1803010l

Maynard, M. T., Mathieu, J. E., Rapp, T. L., & Gilson, L. L. (2012). Something(s) old and

something(s) new: Modeling drivers of global virtual team effectiveness. *Journal of*

Organizational Behavior, 33(3), 342-365. https://doi.org/10.1002/job.1772

Mehta, K., & Shah, V. (2019). Global Business: Virtual Workplace and Collaborations.

International Journal of Business, Humanities and Technology, 9(4), 1-9.

Morrison-Smith, S., & Ruiz, J. (2020). Challenges and barriers in virtual teams: a literature

review. *SN Applied Sciences, 2*, 1096. https://doi.org/10.1007/s42452-020-2801-5

Mysirlaki, S. & Paraskeva, F. (2020). Emotional intelligence and transformational leadership in virtual teams: lessons from MMOGs. *Leadership & Organization Development Journal, 41*(4), 551-566. https://doi.org/10.1108/LODJ-01-2019-0035

Owl Labs (2018). *2018 Global State of Remote Work.* https://resources.owllabs.com/state-of-remote-work/2018#conclusion

Owl Labs (2020). *State of Remote Work.* https://resources.owllabs.com/state-of-remote-work/2020

Pangil, F., & Chan, J. M. (2014). The mediating effect of knowledge sharing on the relationship between trust and virtual team effectiveness. *Journal of Knowledge Management, 18*(1), 92-106. https://doi.org/10.1108/JKM-09-2013-0341

Ross, T. M., Jones, E. C., & Adams, S. G. (2008). Can team effectiveness be predicted? *Team Performance Management, 14*(5/6), 248-268. https://doi-org.ezproxy.ub.unimaas.nl/10.1108/13527590810898518

Schweitzer, L., & Duxbury, L. (2010). Conceptualizing and measuring the virtuality of teams. *Information Systems Journal, 20*(3), 267-295. https://doi.org/10.1111/j.1365-2575.2009.00326.x

Shin, Y. (2004). A person-environment fit model for virtual organizations. *Journal of Management, 30*(5), 725-743. https://doi.org/10.1016/j.jm.2004.03.002

Upwork (2019, March 5). *Third Annual "Future Workforce Report" Sheds Light on How Younger Generations are Reshaping the Future of Work.* https://www.upwork.com/press/releases/third-annual-future-workforce-report

Zeuge, A., Oschinsky, F., Weigel, A., Schlechtinger, M., & Niehaves, B. (2020, August 3-5). *Leading Virtual Teams – A Literature Review* [Paper presentation]. Microsoft 2020 New Future of Work Symposium.

YOUR KNOWLEDGE HAS VALUE